THE Songs OF OUR Heroes VOL. 2

By: **Cynthia Borgueta - Pease**

Preface

His kindness

were it me
the words would be measured
rehearsed
role played
projected
into perfection

but within him
is a boundless wellspring
a wonder of nature
of words, of ideas, of gestures
of easy kindness

that existed through time
generation through generation
gifted to him
to gift to others

and once spoken
every sadness that coursed
through my body
second after second
minute after minute
hour after hour
in this too short life
in this too long life

flowed
at last
forth

I felt my frame rise
I felt my eyes turn

magnetized

awake to his kindness
keen to its readiness

ever hoping to hear it
just once more
then again and again
drift toward me

that
at last
I might be changed

at last
I might be saved.

by: **Bernadette Caballes-Walker**
25th January 2014, 2:45 am

CONTENTS

Definition of Terms:

1. Volunteer
(noun) A person who performs voluntary work
(verb) Agree freely
(adjective) Without payment

2 Office of Standard Education (Ofsted)

Who we are and what we do?
Ofsted is the Office for Standards in Education, Children's Services and Skills. We report directly to Parliament and we are independent and impartial. We inspect and regulate services which care for children and young people, and those providing education and skills for learners of all ages.

Every week, we carry out hundreds of inspections and regulatory visits throughout England, and publish the results on our website. We work with providers which are not yet good to promote their improvement, monitoring their progress and sharing with them the best practice we find.

3 Inspection
Our specialist inspectors are experts in the type of service they inspect. When they carry out an inspection, be it of a children's home, a nursery, a school, a college, or a local authority, they focus on the quality of the service for individual children, young people or older learners. During an inspection, inspectors collect first-hand evidence based on the practice they observe and what they learn from the people using the service. They use this evidence and other information available to make their professional judgements which we publish in inspection reports.

Regulation
For a range of early years and children's social care services, we also act as a regulator, checking that people, premises and the services provided are suitable to care for children and

potentially vulnerable young people. Where childcare or children's social care providers do not meet the required standards, we require them to take the necessary action to improve or do not license them to operate.

In-depth surveys and good practice studies

We also investigate and report on the quality of provision in National Curriculum subjects and aspects of social care, childcare, education, and learning and skills. In these surveys we use our rights of access, and our ability to make expert judgements on the effectiveness of services, to provide unique evidence to local and national policymakers. We share what we find, so those organisations that provide services can learn from what is working well and what is not. And we highlight good practice by publishing reports and individual case studies, drawing on the full range of evidence available.

4 Carer (noun)

1. Person who helps in identifying or preventing or treating illness or disability
2. A person who is responsible for attending to the needs of a child or dependent adult

5 Health Care Assistants Healthcare assistants (HCAs)

HCAs work in hospital or community settings, such as GP surgeries, under the guidance of a qualified healthcare professional. The role can be varied depending upon the healthcare setting.

Most commonly, HCAs work alongside nurses and are sometimes known as nursing auxiliaries or auxiliary nurses. HCAs also work alongside qualified midwives in maternity services.

The types of duties include the following:
- washing and dressing
- serving patients meals and assisting with feeding when necessary

- helping people to mobilise
- toileting
- bed making
- generally assisting with patients' overall comfort
- monitoring patients' conditions by taking temperatures, pulse, respirations and weight

Nursing HCAs usually work a 37.5 hour week on a shift or rota system, typically including nights and weekends. Part-time and flexible working is often available.

Health care practitioners include physicians, dentists, pharmacists (including clinical pharmacists), physician assistants, nurses (including advanced practice registered nurses), midwives (obstetrics), dietitians, therapists, psychologists, chiropractors, clinical officers, social workers, phlebotomists, physical therapists, respiratory therapists, occupational therapists, audiologists, speech pathologists, optometrists, emergency medical technicians, paramedics, medical laboratory scientists, medical prosthetic technicians, radiographers and a wide variety of other human resources trained to provide some type of health care service. They often work in hospitals, health care centres, and other service delivery points, but also in academic training, research, and administration. Some provide care and treatment services for patients in private homes. Many countries have a large number of community health workers who work outside of formal health care institutions. Managers of health care services, health information technicians, and other assistive personnel and support workers are also considered a vital part of health care teams.

Health care practitioners are commonly grouped into five key fields:
1. Medical (including generalist practitioners and specialists);
2. Nursing (including various professional titles);
3. Midwifery (Obstetrics)

4. Dentistry;
5. Other Health Professions, including occupational therapy, pharmacy, physical therapy, paramedicine, respiratory therapy, radiographer and many others health specialists.

6 Residential Homes

Residential care is for people who cannot continue living in their own home, even with support from home care services. You can stay in residential care for a short time (known as respite care), over a longer period or permanently. You would stay in a comfortable furnished room (in some places you could bring your own furniture with you) and staff are available 24 hours a day.

A residential care home normally provides accommodation, meals, and 'personal care'. Personal care can include such things as assistance in getting up or going to bed, eating, washing, dressing, and using the toilet and help with medication administration.

7 Nursing Homes

Nursing Home are best suited for people who require significant personal and nursing care: being bed-bound, having fractures or wounds that are not healing, and having multiple medical problems like diabetes, heart disease and congestive heart failure. Only a quarter of nursing home residents can walk without assistance, and nearly two-thirds receive psychiatric medications. Assisted living facilities are best suited to people with higher levels of functioning and independence who can benefit from social activities, exercise and wellness programs. The main philosophy of assisted living is providing residents with varying levels of choice and independence in a homelike environment

8 National Health Service (NHS)

Since its launch in 1948, the NHS has grown to become the world's largest publicly funded health service. It is also one of the most efficient, egalitarian and comprehensive.

The NHS was born out of a long-held ideal that good healthcare should be available to all, regardless of wealth – a principle that remains at its core. With the exception of some charges, such as prescriptions and optical and dental services, the NHS remains free at the point of use for anyone who is a UK resident. That is currently more than 63.2 million people. It covers everything from antenatal screening and routine treatments for long-term conditions, to transplants, emergency treatment and end-of-life care.

Responsibility for healthcare in Northern Ireland, Scotland and Wales is devolved to the Northern Ireland Assembly, the Scottish Government and the Welsh Assembly Government respectively.

Scale

The NHS employs more than 1.7 milion people. Of those, just under half are clinically qualified – including 39,780 general practitioners (GPs), 370,327 nurses, 18,687 ambulance staff, and 105,711 hospital and community health service (HCHS) medical and dental staff.

Only the Chinese People's Liberation Army, the Wal-Mart supermarket chain and Indian Railways directly employ more people.

The NHS in England is the biggest part of the system by far, catering to a population of 53 million and employing more than 1.35 million people. The NHS in Scotland, Wales and Northern Ireland employs 153,427 – 84,817 and 78,000 people respectively.

The NHS deals with over 1 million patients every 36 hours.

9 Care Quality Commission (CQC)

Its job is to check whether hospitals, care homes, GPs, dentists and services in each and every home in England are meeting national standards.
We do this by inspecting services and publishing our findings, helping people to make choices about the care they receive.

What CQC do
We're the independent health and adult social care regulator.

Its purpose
We make sure health and social care services provide people with safe, effective, compassionate, high-quality care and we encourage them to improve.

Its role
We monitor, inspect and regulate services to make sure they meet fundamental standards of quality and safety and we publish what we find, including performance ratings to help people choose care.

10 Care Quality Commission Inspectors

The compliance inspectors are at the centre of what CQC does. With a wide remit, they are responsible for carrying out planned, follow-up and responsive reviews across a mix of registered providers.

11 Service Unit User: he or she can be a resident confined in a residential or nursing home.

Dedication

I dedicate this book to all those who loves to help others; those who volunteer to help the needy particularly those in war torn areas, those who are helping the victims of calamities, those who help the disadvantaged; the poor. To all the John Does in the whole world who are in these noble works, this is for you.

Acknowledgement

I am forever grateful for the continued help of my two friends-editors who helps edit and proof read the manuscripts for this book. To my former boss in the PDI Visayas, Asst. Editor Irene Sino-Cruz who recently said "Yes!" to help edit the manuscripts; to Mark Ceasar Borgueta-Gariando, my nephew, my lay out artist since the production of The Songs Of The Unsung Heroes Vol 1 and this project, The Songs Of Our Heroes- cheers! I am deeply touched, empowered to do more, to write more inspiring stories because you are with me, helping reach our goals that is to: spread the word of kindness, gratitude and empowerment.

Acknowledged

Introduction

The Spirit of volunteerism or we call it Volunteering here in the United Kingdom, is now the hottest topic if not, most needed "catalyst for change" in this world.

At present, we believe in "The power of voluntary work as a catalyst for change - in individuals, organisations and society as a whole." A title of a group of volunteers doing voluntary works throughout the world, define themselves.

Voluntary works here in the UK are growing in number and they can be found in charity organisations here with at least 160,000 registered groups ready to help those who are in need. These organisations are also in different countries helping those who are victims of calamities, areas which are troubled by conflict, of tragedies.

Oxford Committee for Famine Relief or Oxfam UK , a leading charity in Great Britain was established to help improve the quality of life in most troubled areas started- its charity works started way back in 1940's. Based in its website, it was in 1942, when Oxford Committee for Famine Relief was set up.

In the middle of World War II, the Committee initially lobbied the government for the relaxation of the Allied blockade of occupied Europe, and to ensure the supply of vital relief to civilians, especially in Belgium and Greece.

In 1943, the charity's first appeal launched 'Greek Week' and raised £10,700 for the Greek Red Cross. That's more than £370,000 in current money – an incredible effort from one city in wartime Britain.

'Save Europe Now' campaign launched in 1945 famine committees around the UK – including Oxford – to get behind the campaign to persuade the UK government to allow British nationals to send food parcels to Germany. The first Oxfam shop opened in 1948 at 17 Broad Street in Oxford, which was chosen as the site of the UK's first permanent charity shop. It's still open today – and still depends on our brilliant volunteers.

The Oxford committee almost went global in 1949. As the US Marshall Plan took effect, most of the famine committees around the UK called it a day. However, the Oxford Committee continued its advocacy, boldly pledging to relieve "suffering arising as a result of wars or other causes in any part of the world".

The impact of Ox fam Charity in the troubled areas was soon felt with at least 22,000 volunteers around the world, helping others for about seventy years now. Ox fam is now growing strong.

"Lift one person through Oxfam, and they will lift others. With your help, one good thing leads to another," their website says.

What volunteers say about Ox fam:

 "Every job at Ox fam is a responsible one. I am proud to say that my years here have been among the most rewarding of my career," Barbara, former Chief Executive (taken from www.Oxfam.co.uk)

"I work in a team of about 18 and we all get on really well inside and outside of work. I'm more than aware of how rare that is in a workplace. The upshot is I don't feel like work is a chore at all, even when projects get tough "Mike, Oxford Branch (from **www.Oxfam.co.uk**)

Another registered charity organisation with amazing number of volunteers is the British Heart Foundation. The charity is dedicated to fight heart disease.

The British Heart Foundation's main task is to keep hearts beating even as the foundation remained focus on its research.

"We are UK's number one heart charity and through 50 years of funding cutting edge research, we have already made a big difference to people's lives," the foundation said on its website.

But the landscape of heart disease is changing. More people survive a heart attack or cardiac arrest than ever before, and that means more people are now living with heart disease and need the foundation's help. "As a result we have been reviewing our strategic approach with the help of staff, supporters and stakeholders."

The foundation's new strategy will enable it to lead the fight against cardiovascular disease more effectively. The charity focuses their works on the research projects they funded around UK that aim to fight heart disease, to meet researchers and find out how they have made heart research history.

"We also help people millions of people every year with our up to date information about heart disease so the UK public are better informed," the charity explains on its website. The Heart Foundation Charity also aims to inspire, motivate and help the poor and the under privileged.

Another charity organization, Cancer Research UK Foundation, is the world's leading charity dedicated to cancer research. All the activities of Cancer Research UK are directed towards the charity's ultimate goal of beating cancer through advance research and, raise money to help cancer patients. So far, the foundation has funded over 4,000 researchers, doctors and nurses to meet this goal.

"Our funding covers a wide range of activity, from basic research to late phase clinical trials." This includes drug discovery, basic cell biology, clinical trials, public health, bio marker research and much more.

Based on Cancer Research UK's constitution, the charity will appoint 100 members, who are similar to the shareholders of a company. The members are required to attend all general meetings of Cancer Research UK. Their most significant formal duty is the election of the Trustees.

When Cancer Research UK was formed in 2002, the Trustees, who were the original 20 founding members, appointed 60 more members. At present, the charity has 92 members, including the trustees. Together the members embody a broad range of relevant skills, experience and backgrounds, from business and the arts, politics, finance and health care. They are chosen not to represent particular fields, but as individuals who are supportive of the aims of the charity.

Some of the members were previously associated with the Cancer Research Campaign and the Imperial Cancer Research Fund and because they were enthusiastic in their support of the new charity they were invited to maintain a connection with it.

The others were selected by the new Cancer Research UK Trustee body because of their interest in or knowledge of cancer research and associated health issues and because of their sympathy with the aims of the charity.

"No other charity anywhere in the world is doing more to beat cancer than we are. Including the one that matters most to you, and here in the UK we're the single largest funder of cancer research. All this is only possible with our generous supporters and hard-working scientists," the Cancer Research UK explained. Cancer Research UK has been working on pioneering life-saving research for over a century.

Prince Harry's Aids Foundation " Sentebale "is a charity founded by Prince Harry and Prince of Lesotho, Prince Seeiso. As I go through its web page, I read with profound interest when I encountered these words, "We help the most vulnerable children in Lesotho get the support they need to lead healthy and productive lives."

The charity was founded in 2006 by Prince Harry of the British Royal Family and Prince Seeiso of the Lesotho Royal Family. Prince Harry met Prince Seeiso on his gap year in Lesotho and was moved to help vulnerable children and young people in the country.

Sentebale means 'Forget me not' and the name was chosen "as a memorial to the charity work of our own mothers, as well as a reminder to us all not to forget Lesotho or its children," said Prince Harry when he spoke at the Concert for Diana.

Lesotho has the 3rd highest rate of HIV in the world and there are over 37,000 children under 14 living with HIV. The country has 360, 000 orphans and around 10% of all children are vulnerable.

Sentebale aims to combat these issues and works with vulnerable children and their communities, empowering them to reach their full potential. The charity is focused on community-led development which matches actual need. [Prince Harry's Aids Foundation which is named "Sentebale" focus on the people of Kingdom of Lesotho, which has a population of 2.2 million. The kingdom has an estimated 360,000 orphans. Thirteen percent of the kingdom's children are vulnerable; their rights to survival and development are not being met. The kingdom's life expectancy is on average just 41.2 years

The country has the third highest rate of HIV/AIDS in the world. In the country, knowledge about HIV prevention is low. The two most common misconceptions on HIV/AIDS in Lesotho are that a person can become infected through mosquito bites or sharing food. In Lesotho, only 38% of women and 29% of men age 15-49 have comprehensive knowledge about HIV/AIDS. Among youth, this figure is 39% for women and 29% for men.

Sentebale works with local grass roots organisations to help these children – the victims of extreme poverty and Lesotho's

HIV/AIDS epidemic. The words such as: Together, we're making a big difference to these children's lives attracts me the most as they connotes a vow to eradicate extreme poverty in Lesotho,Africa. The foundation's call for help: We can do even more with your help, is a clear signal of a strong commitment from its founder.

The foundation's priority is always to reach Lesotho's most needy and vulnerable children, many of whom are the victims of extreme poverty and Lesotho's HIV/AIDS epidemic.

The foundation's aim is to direct aid through funding and management support to voluntary, grass roots community services that attempt to fill the gaps in care. Whether they offer vulnerable children safe accommodation, hot meals or psychosocial support, these services can make a huge difference to children's ability to lead a more rewarding life. The foundation is also considering more entrepreneurial projects that can change the lives of communities trying to support vulnerable children.

In the next chapters of this book, I take pride to present, encourage the spirit of voluntary works being shared by these special, inspiring, empowered individuals whose idealism and dedication to help others made them what and who they are to others. It can best explain that they were inspired by the growing number of charity works they see around them. Who and what inspired them to do the same can be attributed to their forefathers, loved ones, role models they had set for themselves. Let us see and read why there is a very strong connection why these 'catalyst for change' is embraced by these special individuals I included for this book. I believe that the existing charities operating worldwide to uplift the lives of others have something to do with their dedication to be there for others in their time of need.

PART I

STORIES AS TOLD TO THE AUTHOR

1 - EMILY RUTTERFORD

2 - IAN GALLAGHER

3 - JOANNA SILARSKA

4 - THOMAS HAMILTON

Chapter 1
MRS. EMILY RUTTERFORD

Retired Teacher, Community Organiser

(Photo courtesy of Eastern Daily Press or EDP and through www.GreatCressingham.com) Mrs Emily Rutterford with Great Cressingham Parish Council chairman Michael Halls during the opening ceremony and Installation of the children's play equipment in Village Green in 2013.

Eighty-six-year old Emily, who lives alone in her house in Great Cressingham Thetford, Norfolk, looks radiant in spite of her age. As she let me inside her huge house, I see a woman beaming with happiness, with pride and with a kind-hearted nature. She is simply looking her best.

Emily is a mother of three children, all of whom are all professionals and are doing well in their chosen fields. She explained that her children's accomplishment could be attributed to her and her husband's presence during their children's formative years. "We are simply hands-on parents. We are just doing our best to simply being there for them when they need us."

Emily spent almost all her adult life teaching elementary graders in the different schools of East Anglia but she is also into community organising. "These two are very rewarding for me. When I am teaching and I knew that my students has improved, it made me feel proud not because of what I have done for them but mainly because of the value of education and what it would do for their future."

Over and above teaching her pupils various subjects, Emily also taught them the importance of saving and handling money. "I remember how I would go out my way to be with my pupils in going to the bank. I showed them how to deposit their money, how to withdraw, I taught them the basics."

Emily also took time to provide advice to her students and their parents. "There was a time a mother of my student came to me crying, asking what can be done so her daughter can enrol in the course she wanted her to study. I just told the mother that her child is good in Art and that it would be better to choose Fine Arts or Fashion Design because it was in this field her daughter was good at. I was surprised to know years later that this daughter of hers is now one of the designers of a prominent magazine in the world."

She urged parents to determine the strengths and interests of their children and allow them to pursue these. "If your child can't add up or is slow in some subjects but is good in other field of study, you have to encourage him or her to pursue where they are good at. This way, they would be successful in the future," she explained.

Emily also noted that a teacher has to consider the educational needs of their students and at the same, provide recognition of their accomplishments. "You teach according to the needs of the learner. When you see them excel or good in one or more subjects, let the child know about it. Acknowledge how good they are in it."

When asked who inspired her to become a teacher, she readily said, "My parents.

Emily maintained that the things she learned from her parents helped her chose teaching as a career. "I am simply passing on the ideals I learned from them to my pupils, and even now, to my grandchildren. It was rewarding and full of fun and I love every minute I spent while teaching. I felt accomplished when my students learned what I taught them inside the class. When after a series of lessons for example, my students can clearly illustrate what they learned and are able to graduate or finish school with honours, then I am fulfilled."

When their students finish their studies, especially if they graduate with honours from school, teachers feel proud, she pointed out. "It is like our legacy to them."

Emily, who was honed by her parents to help those who are in need, also spends some of her time doing good deeds for people in need and helping fund raising activities. Her efforts to help have not gone unnoticed. She is usually approached to help someone in need in the village or in the neighbouring areas. She is also a favorite choice among persons tapped to organise a fete to raise funds for a noble project in their village or to just be present when others need moral support.

"I was glad to help. This practice has been carried out in their family, from generation to generation," she pointed out.

Emily's parents both hailed from Great Cressingham, Thetford England. Her father worked as a Home Guard during Second World War. "He was assigned to watch the village, its residents, watching the aircrafts leaving and when they are coming.

Long after the war ended, her father continued to work in the Army. As her family owns a vast land, her dad cultivated their property and later helped managed the farm. Her mother, a housewife, was always busy taking care of the family's wellbeing.

When she got married, Emily passed on the same practice to her offspring. "How I was brought up was also the same upbringing I instilled to my children. I was brought up to help others...it is a family thing for me." She said her eldest son is kept busy with managing their farm and helping in parish activities, being the Vice-Chairman of the village pastoral council.

Emily also loves to bake cakes, make jams and bread and sells them for a cause whenever there is a village fete or car boot as a means to raise funds.

Her advocacy to help others is well known that when I started asking the locals in Great Cressingham who among the residents is worthy enough to be mentioned and be honoured for this book project, many of them mentioned her name to me saying: Mrs Emily Rutterford, you should see and include her!

Chapter 2
●·····················●
IAN GALLAGHER

Team Leader & Employment Coordinator –
Action for Blind People (Norfolk)

Ian Gallagher had been involved in charity work long before he decided to move to another charity organization, the Action for Blind People, on October 2007. Ian was working for another charity supporting adults with learning difficulties and mental and physical issues with gaining employment.

Ian was an employment coordinator when he found out about Action. "It just hit me and I decided right there and then to join the group as I find their work fulfilling," he said. It was when he attended a training he learned what Action for Blind People is for.

"I wanted a new challenge and was impressed with the great work Action For Blind People does," explained Ian.

The Action for Blind People is an expert national charity organisation, with local reach, catering to blind and partially sighted people get practical support in all aspects of their lives.

The organisation offers support with day to day living, welfare rights, housing issues, and managing personal budgets. They offer tailored support in all aspects of life after sight loss, enabling the blind and partially sighted to make informed choices and to be in control of the way they want to live their life and maintain independence.

They also provide community based course for people who are just newly diagnosed with sight loss and how to increase confidence levels.

In terms of money, Action provides financial advice service about welfare rights including personal budgets as part of self-directed support, same in housing issues and so when one needs a companion when they travel or go shopping, the group has dedicated team providing practical support.

"I, for one can attest that Action listens and get their support when I needed it. They sent me two people to listen to my concerns as I am partially sighted and needed advice in terms of some issues," Ian recalls.

It was at this time when I came to know Ian. Although he has eye sight problems, he is efficient in his job. Although he's been suffering from Glaucoma for years now, his eyesight is still good.

Ian drives his own car and it helps him to arrive on time to meet a client. "I will always be working even if I became fully blind," he stressed. "It is here I find to meet different kinds of people with different, unique needs."

The organisation stated on its website that there are around 360,000 people who are registered blind or partially sighted in the United Kingdom. Of this number 299,000 are in England, 34,500 are in Scotland, 16,000 in Wales and 8,000 in Northern Ireland.

Quoting Access Economics, the Action for Blind People further stated that the number of people with sight loss in UK is expected to increase considerably to almost four million by 2050. By 2020, the number of people with sight loss in UK, with its ageing population, will rise to over 2,250,000 as the prevalence of sight loss increases with age. Obesity and diabetes also causes sight loss, the group added.

The United Kingdom spends at least £2.3 billion in 2009/2010 in healthcare expenditure related to eye health. This amount included inpatient and outpatient treatment costs as well as the cost of the eye tests funded by the UK National Health System. However, the amount did not cover other costs, including those related to research and development.

In April 2009, Action for Blind People became part of Royal National Institute for Blind People (RNIB), in an innovative partnership combining regional service delivery across England. This partnership enables both organisations to share skills and deliver services in line with the UK Vision strategy.

Before he joined the Action for Blind People, Ian, who is in his mid-40s, was a training and employment consultant of Meridian East of the Broadland Housing Association from 2005 to 2007. Meridian East helps people living in Broadland Housing property who are not employed, explore work options and provide employment-related training needs.

Chapter 3

JOANNA SILARSKA

Health Care Assistant. A caring daughter and loving wife.

Becoming a care giver is not just a job but a calling because this requires dedication, compassion and understanding of the needs of the client.

I have known Joanna for almost seven years now. She works as a Health Care Assistant in the same care home I am working. As a carer, Joanna is dedicated to her job and I can attest to the fact that she loves her job.

Joanna is one of the few carers I knew since I arrived here in England in September 2007. Joanna hails from Poland. She spent her early childhood in Szczecin, Poland where she finished an Occupational Therapy course.

Hard working and heedful of the resident's needs, Joanna is well-liked not only by the residents and their families but also by her coworkers and who would not? "Caring comes natural, easy to find in her," a lady resident often times told me.

"She is very dedicated to her job," Grace, former carer now kitchen assistant in the same work place agreed.

There are at least twenty carers in our workplace. Although there are carers who are more senior than Joanna, I find her the best in providing care to our residents at the home. Why? Because she sees to it that her resident's needs are met. I have seen her never failing to answer whenever the buzzer rings. The residents use this tool (buzzer) whenever they need help. Unlike other carers who don't respond to the ringing of the buzzer and choose to ignore the call for help, she is the first one to see, to determine who is needing assistance.

Of course, there are also other carers who are good but they are not as dedicated to their jobs as Joanna, said another co - worker who does not want to be named.

One may ask what is the difference between caring for our loved ones and being a carer or a Health Care Assistant in a hospital or in a nursing home?

I would say, none at all. Taking care of a loved one or loved ones or caring somebody is spontaneous, unconstrained an act of love.

I googled the definition of carer and it says: A carer (noun) is a person who helps in identifying or preventing or treating illness or disability; or, A carer is a person who is responsible for attending to the needs of a child or dependent adult.

The word care (verb) is defined as feel concern or interest; or, look after; give medial or emotional help.

The word alone, means so much to reckon with, particularly, if this is asked in a work place like a care home. I heard a resident say: Yeah right, this is supposedly a care home but where is the care? This is not a home at all. Much more for a care home, a teary eyed resident said.

If one is a care provider, he or she should possess the capability to extend care in its truest meaning. Caring is a tough job that requires a lot of patience and a lot of tender, loving care.

This is more profound if the carer is working in the hospital or in a care home where he or she is bound to the mandate and policies of the workplace.

The question now is: Does caring for the sick in care homes different from caring for those who are in their respective homes or those who are admitted in the hospitals? Are the sick being treated with dignity, respect they deserve when they are confined in care homes? What is the quality of care for a patient confined in a nursing/residential home?

The Care Quality Commission (CQC)

The Care Quality Commission (CQC) is the independent regulator of health and social care in England.

CQC also protect the interests of people whose rights are restricted under the Mental Health Act.

Whether services are provided by the NHS, local authorities, private companies or voluntary organisations, we make sure that people get better care. CQC do this by:

- Driving improvement across health and social care.

- Putting people first and championing their rights.

- Acting swiftly to remedy bad practice.

- Gathering and using knowledge and expertise, and working with others.

It is their job to ensure that all health and social care services meet essential standards of quality and safety, and that they give people a good experience of care. The new system of registration will play a key role in helping them to do this.

Upon registration of these health care facilities, the web site added that all services will have to show that they meet the same standards of quality and safety – whether they are provided in a person's home, in the community or in a hospital, and irrespective of how the care is funded and whether it is acute care or longer-term residential care.

CQC will continually monitor and check compliance with the new standards, to make sure that potential problems are identified early. "We will ensure that quick action is taken if a service is failing the people who use it."

Reports said there is a widespread abuse happening in the different health care facilities here in England. CQC reports said ten percent failed to exercise their duties to protect these vulnerable people.

"CQC inspectors carried out more than 35,000 inspections in 2012-2013. In around 90% of cases people were treated with dignity and respect and were receiving care, treatment and support that meet their needs and was safe. But despite improvements in each type of care setting, we are disappointed that around ten percent of cases received poor quality of care."

CQC listed a number of health providers, which failed in this aspect every year.

Some patients, as well as residents/service unit users are not happy with the way they are being treated inside their care homes or in the hospitals. However, many, particularly the families of the residents, has turned a blind eye to this, saying they are happy nonetheless as they have seen that their loved ones' well-being are being looked after, which would not have been the case if they just stay alone in their homes.

If and when a service unit user or resident or their families are not happy with the services given by the care homes or hospitals and or by their staff, the family of the affected residents or those who witnessed the violations have always the options to file a complaint with the CQC in writing.

When you see that your loved ones needs are neglected and ignored, when the recipient or "service user" failed to receive a need to be cared for, such as residents were not given proper hygiene, food, being maltreated, these violations of the human rights and these bad practices must be reported to the CQC.

"The rights of the vulnerable people both in their respective homes or in a facility are strongly monitored, taken care of," the CQC guidelines further said.

To provide excellent care, the carer must have the virtue of patience, love, perseverance. If these qualities are present in a health care assistant, then the recipient or the one they are caring for will live longer, their patients bodies flourished.

Joanna as Best Carer

One thing that makes her stand out from the rest of her colleagues is that she gives her best when at work. All the more I respect her when I came to know that she was once working as a volunteer in Poland before moving here in the UK. I know how it is to do volunteering works. You work without getting paid of the services you do. Joanna is no exemption to the rest of volunteers doing free service to others.

"At one part of my life (2000 or 2001) I was looking after an older man who was on a wheelchair. I was going to his house two days a week (he was living with his wife) for 3 or 4 hours. I cared for him. I was helping him go to the toilet. I was making drinks and meals for him. I was giving him things he could not take himself. I listened to him, we were chatting and I was also cleaning his house. It lasted a couple of weeks," Joanna recalled.

During her internship at the occupational therapy workshop, Joanna organised activities for disabled people and was also responsible for their personal needs such as giving them a bath and changing their clothes, among others.

When she was doing her vocational training in Medical and Social Workers she worked in two different nursing and residential homes.

"I was responsible for organising different activities for the residents in these homes although they were mostly manual things. But what the residents appreciated the most, was the attention I gave to them. I chat, walk or just sit with them. It was here when I realised that what people need the most, is our presence. They want our attention. This helps them a lot," she said.

She also looked after children. She first took care of Julia when she was 20 months old. Next, came Paul who was 11 months old and Miron who was then six months old. I looked after Julia for six months. My babysitting for Paul lasted only for two months.

Joanna then worked in a factory. "But this job really did not satisfy me. I really wanted to work with disabled people because this satisfies me. I worked in different places with disabled children and the elderly. I had to stop working in my place after I got an offer to work here in the UK."

It helps that Joanna is well-trained in health and social care as she obtained a Level 2 National Vocational Course (NVQ). This qualification is designed for those who support and assist individuals with their physical or emotional care, daily living needs or maintaining their independence. It is extremely relevant for home care assistants, community support assistants, healthcare assistants and residential or day service assistants. The course focuses around person-enabled care, in the development and maintenance of individual independence and direct care delivery to the service users.

As she is also one of the activity coordinator in the care home, her passion on crafting, art, cooking and, of music made her all the more closer to the residents she is taking care of. "As I told you, Cynthia, I am more comfortable if I know Joanna is here," a lady resident repeatedly said.

Chapter 4
THOMAS HAMILTON

Parole and Probation Volunteer

Thomas Hamilton came from Scotland to settle down in Tacloban City, Philippines upon his retirement in April 15, 2005. He then joined the Lions Club International, Tacloban chapter.

"I joined this organisation as this international group is focused on serving the local needy people, with its medical missions, feeing and providing assistance to those who are victims of calamities. I feel the passion to do the same," said Thomas.

His decision to join the Lions Club International is not surprising since he has been involved in volunteer works for years. "My involvement in volunteer works dates back many years but to be truly committed to this did not happen until I retired and had time to devote to this cause."

His membership in the Lions Club International led to another involvement in volunteer work. "It was here when I met a fellow member who invited me to attend a seminar run by the Parole and the Probation Deparment. The outcome of this was that it led me to become a member in the Volunteer Parole Aide (VPA) programme," Thomas recalled.

The VPA program, created under the Presidential Decree No. 968, which mandated the employment of Volunteer Probation Aides to assist the provincial or city probation officers in the supervision of probationers. The VPAs, who don't receive any regular compensation for services except for reasonable travel allowance, are appointed for two years, which could be extended based on their performance.

The programme received a boost when former President Gloria Macapagal Arroyo signed executive number 468 on October 11, 2005. E.O. 468 aimed to strengthen community involvement and participation in crime prevention, treatment of offenders and the administration of criminal justice.

The VPAs serve as strengths and role models so they could promote reformation of offenders who become members of their own communities. They also help improve the rehabilitation prospect of offenders by helping them in looking for jobs, schooling, training opportunities and other activities.

He never regretted his decision to become a VPA. "Nine years on, I am happy with what I am doing, realising that it is a noble work to be helping others this way," Thomas explained.

Becoming a VPA was quite challenging for Thomas. "I often reflect how it was possible for me to be living in this country with a complete different culture, different attitude to life, eventually, it was a yes that I was accustomed to liking this country, its people. Just imagine here I was in a country with a completely different culture, different attitude to life and I was asked to report on parolees and probationers now this is what I called a challenge!"

The VPAs undergo basic training course to give them knowledge on the agency and its programs and services and participate in team building designed to reinforce the values of cooperation and trust. They also had to undergo specialized training to provide them knowledge and skills on restorative justice, therapeutic community, interviewing skills, reports preparation, and community resource development, among others.

"After some training and seminars on the law about parolees, I was allocated three clients to supervise," Thomas said.

His first client had done 17 years in prison for murder; the second had served 12 years for armed robbery and the third had 10 years for manslaughter. "At first, I did not know what to expect; I just went do what I had to do," he recalled.

"First, I had to see the local community leader and introduced myself and what I was planning to do within his area; then off to see the clients at their homes. Remembering how it was then, it was certainly a challenge!"

After two months in it, I started to relax and enjoy this voluntary work. Getting to know them; giving advice on the problems they faced, in fact, I started to respect their commitment to comply with their parole conditions. I believe they did benefit with my personal supervision thus it also made me think it is a good feeling to be helping others. A good cause indeed!

After three years, having more trainings to equip myself in helping my clients, I focused more on being a facilitator, helping them acquire skills, improve their quality of life to generate income for their families.

When I first joined the VPA's, we were based inTacloban now this was a very new project. I found out very quickly that many volunteers were doing this for their own agenda, such as political or a position within their barangay. I approached the regional director if I could recruit volunteers in Tanauan, Leyte (where my partner is based) and form a cluster so we can only just focus on Tanauan.

After several weeks, this was granted. We recruited 15 people and organized their training and I must admit from the beginning these volunteers were great to work with as right from the start they did several small fund raising projects.

One of the volunteers, Jane Pingal, donated the use of a small bamboo and nipa cottage for a training center so we can use it as a reporting center for our clients. This gave us the chance to arrange livelihood skill seminars. Also, one of the earlier seminars was on hydroponics, growing lettuce and others.

We latter lost Jane, a great person and a great friend. She died along with 16 of her family members, when Yolanda (Haiyan) swept away her house.

After Yolanda destroyed his house in Tanauan, Leyte. Thomas decided to move to Manila, Philippines.

PART II

STORIES WRITTEN BY CONTRIBUTORS

Chapter 5

•·····································•
Prof. ROLANDO O. BORRINAGA, Ph.D.

School of Health Sciences
University of the Philippines Manila
Palo, Leyte

Super-typhoon Yolanda
(International code name Haiyan):
The new milestone of our lives

When typhoon Yolanda (Haiyan) made landfall several times in central Philippines on November 8, 2013, it caused the death of thousands and left massive devastation along its path.

When Yolanda struck, the winds it carried destroyed all the buildings inside the campus of the UP Manila School of Health Sciences in Palo, Leyte, where I teach. Although the storm surge waters did not reach the *poblacion* (town proper), most of the buildings in town, including the newly renovated Palo Cathedral, were destroyed. A number of our students who live in barangays (villages) south of the town swam in storm surge waters, but luckily they survived.

There were no Yolanda casualties among my colleagues and students. As for our students, they might have been victims themselves in their boarding houses, but they promptly teamed up as front-line first aid workers in the church convent and municipal building in Palo who catered to the needs of hundreds of people needing immediate care for the injuries they suffered during the ordeal. In fact, one of our nursing students from Mindanao attended to the breech delivery of a birthing mother "on the road," so to speak, while they were serially transporting her through the debris-filled highway for appropriate care from Palo to a Tacloban hospital.

In days immediately after Yolanda, there was a dearth of information, only those we got from DZRH-Manila and the Cebu radio stations as well as word of mouth through our neighbors, friends and acquaintances in the streets. I could not use my cellphone until about 10 days after the event, when some weak signals returned and I had my unit recharged somewhere. But I had to do the texting at night on the roof of my house, within sight and hearing of the sustained drones of C-130 cargo planes flying in and out of Tacloban airport, bringing in relief items from all over world. I read only two newspaper issues during those initial weeks, brought in by my Cebu-based son who travelled home twice to bring much-needed relief items and maintenance medicines.

I was able to watch TV and access the Internet again 38 days after Yolanda, when my wife and I traveled to Cebu for a few days of much-needed break and relaxation. For symbolic reasons, I would have wanted to travel out 40 days or more after the event, but we did not want to be caught up by the Christmas rush to travel back home from Cebu.

My wife and I did not join the exodus of thousands of refugees that fled Tacloban and nearby areas on board C-130 cargo planes and other forms of transportation toward Manila or Cebu in the days after Yolanda. Our choice to stay was deliberate. Inspired by my favorite author, the late 19th-century American naturalist and transcendentalist philosopher Henry David Thoreau, I took the chance "to front only the essential facts of life," to learn what it had to teach after Yolanda drove it into a corner and simplified and reduced it to its lowest terms (Thoreau 1993, 75). I kept a daily diary of the first six months after Yolanda, but I still have to process which was mean or which was sublime about the entire experience.

As a local historian, I view natural disasters in our region both as historical processes and as sequential events. As historical processes, the data I had gathered for Eastern Visayas suggest that these disasters follow some pattern or cycle over long periods of time, the type that fall under Fernand Braudel's category of *longue durée* or the long-term duration (en.wikipedia.ord/wiki/Fernand_Braudel).

However, the wider, integrative theoretical perspective that I subscribe to remains unpopular among many social scientists, most of whom still view disasters as discrete, non-sequential historical events (Bankoff 2004, 24).

Comparing Yolanda and the typhoon that hit Tacloban City on October 12-13, 1897, it could be established that Yolanda followed almost the exact path of the 1897 typhoon. Just like Yolanda, the 1897 typhoon had the same path passing across Leyte Gulf after it made landfall in Samar. In Leyte province, the 1897 typhoon's storm surges reached three meters in Tanauan; 3.9 meters in Tacloban city proper and 4.6 meters in the city's Anibong District. On the other hand, the storm surges reached 4.9 meters in Basey, five meters in Marabut town, three meters in Guiuan and 7.3 meters , all in Samar island, (Algue 1898, 30A). I had inquired about and checked the average surge water heights from Yolanda in several areas around Tacloban, and I had come to the conclusion that the storm surge here in 1897 was at least half-meter higher than that of last November. (Please check this paragraph with Professor Borrinaga as the figures on storm surge might be that of Yolanda not the 1897 typhoon)

Although TV and newspaper reports had claimed that Supertyphoon Yolanda or Haiyan was the strongest typhoon to ever fall on land in recorded history, this is not quite true anymore. The evidence shows that the 1897 typhoon that Yolanda replicated 116 years later was stronger. There were no measures yet for kilometers or miles per hour winds in 1897, but they already had barometric measures, which tell that a lower reading indicates a stronger typhoon. Yolanda's ten-minute sustained winds of 230 km/h (145 mph) had the equivalent intensity of 895 mbar in the barometer (en.wikipedia.ord/Typhoon Haiyan – Wikipedia, the free encyclopedia.htm), but the 1897 typhoon registered barometric readings below 760 mbar (Algue 1898, 65A). I still have to inquire from experts the equivalent of this low barometric reading in kilometers or miles per hour winds.

The 1897 typhoon caused the death of about 200 people or 2.5% of Tacloban's estimated population of 8,000 at the time (Algue 1898, 38). Yolanda's official death count for Tacloban is about 3,000, or about 1.4% of its 210,000 population, but independent observers place the number of deaths here around 5,000, with a percentage that matches the 1897 figure (Personal communication with Tacloban Vice-Mayor Jerry T. Yaokasin).

The pattern of physical destruction brought about by the two typhoons more than a century apart presents some visual similarities. For instance, an 1897 photograph showing the damaged church and municipal building in Palo town was visually similar to the extent of damage on both buildings last November. I took the recent photo from the approximate area on a Palo hill where the camera man presumably took his photo in 1897.

A part of Tacloban where I rendered extension work in the past is Anibong District, its oldest slum area. I coordinated a community survey here in 1987 for a Rotary Club project and the findings showed that in an area of about one-third square kilometer, there lived 4,285 people in six barangays (Borrinaga 1988, 5). When Yolanda struck last November, the houses on the seaward side of Paseo de Legazpi, the street that runs through the length of the district, were all washed out. Yet the number of deaths due to the storm surge here was only around 100. A portion of these deaths were caused by five large cargo boats that plowed through the houses on the northern part of

Anibong, pushed there by the storm surge waters. A schooner with two masts was also photographed to have been beached around the area by the storm surge in 1897.

Most of the deaths from the storm surge in Tacloban were from the barangays of San Jose District on the Cataisan Peninsula, where the airport is located. The flattened and debris-piled landscapes in this area were best featured by the TV networks, newspapers, magazines, and social media in the early days after Yolanda, when many other parts of the city were still virtually hard to reach by deadline-pressed journalists and security-conscious visiting prominent officials.

The 1899 Map of Leyte (USCGS) shows that Cataisan Peninsula was a swampy place almost detached from its village named *Casiruman*, which literally means "a place of darkness." The place assumed importance during World War II, when both the Japanese and the Allied Forces that displaced them tried to develop an airport here. In the post-war years, the airport became a magnet for commerce and residence in the peninsula such that, in recent decades, San Jose District had become one of the most densely populated areas of Tacloban.

Largely forgotten in due course was the changing of the village's name from *Casiruman*, a place of darkness, to San Jose, a Christian name. The change of names was apparently influenced by the deadly aftermath of the storm surge carried by the 1897 typhoon. In the 1903 Census, San Jose had replaced the name *Casiruman* in the official documents, the first place given a Christian name in the history of Tacloban. This singular erasure of a piece of collective memory, which word meaning served as a clear warning itself, would have fatal consequences when Yolanda reprised the forgotten previous disaster.

The peninsula's name itself, *Cataisan*, literally means "the sharpest point." As a geographic feature, this former thick mangrove swamp must have gradually evolved and functioned as natural buffer zone and first line of defense of *Cancabatoc*, the old name of Tacloban, against long-term cycles of storm surges in the past. That it became a killing field for Yolanda should teach us some hard lessons about factoring the environment and the impact of climate change on our lives starting now.

In the aftermath of Yolanda, there arose a debate on what is the Filipino term for storm surge. In the immediate days before November 8, when this phenomenon was announced as a possibility, the experts disagreed to call it tsunami, because it is not triggered by an earthquake. After the disaster, the native term for storm surge remained elusive. The debate even landed in the pages of the *Philippine Daily Inquirer*. Since it can never be called tsunami, different proponents submitted such terms as *"tsu-balod," "tsu-alon," "silakbô," "daluyong," "humbak,"* and even *"Tacloban."* I joined in by arguing that the forgotten ancient word appropriate for this tidal phenomenon is *"karak-an"* (*PDI*, January 26, 2014, A16). The debate remains unresolved.

In these days of mega-disasters, we are best advised to study and understand past patterns or cycles of the recent disasters that struck Mindanao and the Visayas, right down to our respective provinces and towns, so that we can be better prepared to cope and deal with the forthcoming ones.

After Bohol and Cebu were struck by a Magnitude 7.2 earthquake on October 15, 2013, which destroyed many towns and heritage churches in Bohol, it very briefly crossed my mind that it might be followed by an event similar to the 1897 typhoon in Samar and Leyte. But I thought this was mere fancy. After all, when a Magnitude 6.9 earthquake struck Guihulngan in Negros Oriental on February 6, 2012, an accompanying a false "tsunami alert" created much panic in Cebu City that forced residents to flee to higher grounds.

While browsing the Internet last February in Cebu, where they have strong signal not yet available in Tacloban, during my second trip there after Yolanda, I came across an item in rappler.com about the two strongest earthquakes that ever rocked the Philippines in 1897. The epicenters of these tremors were in the Celebes Sea area west of Mindanao. The first on September 20, 1897 registered a magnitude of 8.6 in the Richter scale, and the second a day later registered a magnitude of 8.7 (www.rappler.com/MAP Strongest earthquakes in the Philippines.htm). What I had known before from my research was that one earthquake (most likely the second of the two) triggered tsunamis that slammed into the coastal areas of Negros, Panay and Palawan.

Then the insight flashed that there were uncanny parallels between the twin disasters of 1897 and 2013, respectively. Call it plain coincidence or non-sequential, but only three weeks (21 days) separated the strongest earthquake to have rocked the Philippines on September 21, 1897 and my proposed strongest typhoon to ever fall on land on October 12, 1897. And the same three weeks period (24 days) separated the Bohol earthquake on October 15, 2013 and Supertyphoon Yolanda on November 8, 2013.

A third parallelism is the fact that Tacloban and Capiz were reference points for both the 1897 typhoon and Yolanda in Leyte and Panay, respectively.

There also parallels of Typhoon Sendong in December 2011 and Typhoon Pablo in December 2012 in Mindanao close to the twin disasters in 1897? My friend, Dr. Antonio Montalvan

II of Cagayan de Oro City, who writes a column in the *Philippine Daily Inquirer*, had claimed that there were in fact some strong typhoons that struck the so-called typhoon-free Mindanao in the years close to 1897.

The unfortunate thing is that the historical narratives for 1897 in our textbooks are largely focused on the events of the Philippine Revolution being fought in Luzon. We do not find any mention of the record-breaking natural disasters that threatened the lives of hundreds of thousands of people in Mindanao and the Visayas at the time, and even claimed the lives of many. The fact that these disasters occurred toward the end of the century, or *fin de siècle* as the French called it, must have instilled a lot of fear among our people that the world was going to end in 1900. But it seems these violent acts of nature then had to be ignored in favor of the social dynamics involving human actors who think they can move the nation and dictate the course of history.

In the weeks and few months after Yolanda, when our school operations were suspended and the students had been sent home, when there was not much work to do, when there was no electricity yet in the house (until four months later), and there was much time for boredom and waiting for the overall social services situation in Tacloban to stabilize, I decided to catch up on my book readings. Around the disaster's half-year mark last month (May), I finished reading Leo Tolstoy's monumental epic, *War and Peace*, which was set during Napoleon Bonaparte's invasion of Russia in 1812. Although I had read the book's two epilogues with the author's treatise on history more than 30 years ago, reading the entire story this time around provided a fascination of its own. It helped me put in context the bickering of our politicians and "great men" types who think they have control and can dictate the pace of post-Yolanda recovery and rehabilitation efforts.

Tolstoy wrote: "Examining only those expressions of the will of historical personages which were related to events as commands, historians have assumed that the events depended on the commands. But examining the events themselves and the connection in which the historical persons stood to the people, we have found that they and the commands were dependent on events" (Tolstoy 1998, 1289).

The finger-pointing over the blame for the confusion and anarchy, the looting of business establishments, and the exodus of people away from Tacloban that were linked to the vacuum or failure of leadership in the few days after Yolanda simply underscored the dependence of our leaders and their acts on the natural course of this disaster. I strongly believe that a similar cycle of human reactions happened in the wake of the 1897 typhoon, but unfortunately the chroniclers of that time were silent about this.

About "great men" types, Tolstoy wrote: "In historic events, the so-called great men are labels giving names to events, and like labels they have but the smallest connection with the event itself. Every act of theirs, which appears to them an act of their own will, is in an historical sense involuntary, and is related to the whole course of history and predestined from eternity" (*Ibid.*, 648-649).

The greatest bane in the post-Yolanda recovery and rehabilitation efforts are the image-building tactics of some local leaders to impose their names as labels and simultaneously spite their political adversaries on specific aspects of these efforts. The credit-grabbing dynamics are being rationalized by partisans in gossip circles as practical realities of local politics. Some of them seem to be succeeding, to the detriment of their less-favored constituents. Of some consolation to the unaligned majority of Yolanda victims, independent international and national NGOs have filtered down parallel assistance and are making significant successes in their own efforts, even under the shadow of petty politics.

On the force that moves nations, Tolstoy wrote: "The movement of nations is caused not by power, nor by intellectual activity, nor even by a combination of the two as historians have supposed, but by the activity of *all* the people who participate in the events, and who always combine in such a way that those taking the largest direct share in the event take on themselves the least responsibility and vice-versa" (*Ibid.*, 1290).

There is a need for educators to engage in the "least responsibility" of introducing and teaching about the environment and climate change impacts as components of the New General Education Curriculum. The resulting "critical mass" of their collective efforts can greatly contribute to the body of actionable knowledge that could help cushion or prevent the adverse consequences of future disasters in your respective places of origin.

Whether we like it or not, the tragic images produced by Supertyphoon Yolanda, now recorded and available in the public domain, will likely haunt and influence the movement of our nation and the conduct of our leaders and our people over the next few years. Along this line, the Post-Haiyan Tacloban Declaration on disaster risk reduction and management, which came out of the Asia-Europe Meeting held in Manila last June 4-6, 2014, already provides revised policy directions and guideposts for the international community in dealing with mega-disasters over the next decade or so (www.rappler.com/Post-Haiyan-Tacloban-Declaration.htm).

In Tacloban City itself, Supertyphoon Yolanda has already become the new milestone of our lives.

Author's photo: Taken during the 153rd Naval Pueblo Day

References

Alcina, Francisco Ignacio, SJ. *Historia de las islas e indios de Bisayas* ... 1668. Part I,
Book 2 of the Alcina manuscripts has been translated to English and published. See Kobak, Cantius J., OFM, and Lucio Gutierrez, OP (eds.). *History of the Bisayan People in the Philippine Islands*, Part I, Vol. 2. Manila: UST Publishing House, 2004.

Algue, Jose S.J. *El Baguio de Samar y Leyte, 12-13 de Octubre de 1897*. Manila:
>Observatorio de Manila, 1898.

Artigas, Manuel Cuerva. *Reseña de la Provincia de Leyte*. Manila: Imprenta "Cultura Filipina," 1914.

Bankoff, Greg. "Time is of the Essence: Disasters, Vulnerability and History."
International Journal of Mass Emergencies and Disasters XXII: 3 (November 2004): 23-42.

Borrinaga, Rolando O. "A Profile of an Urban Slum in Tacloban, Leyte, Philippines."
>*Leyte-Samar Studies* XXII: 1&2 (1988): 1-40.

_____. "A history of geologic collapses in St. Bernard," *Philippine Daily Inquirer*,
>February 25, 2006, p. A14.

_____. "Volcano scare in Biliran," *Philippine Daily Inquirer*, December 1, 2007, p.
>A16.

_____. "Rising from the Destruction of UP SHS by Supertyphoon 'Yolanda':
Learning from History," *UP Forum*, November-December 2013, pp. 1-3.

_____. "'Karak-an' is appropriate word," *Philippine Daily Inquirer*, January 26,
>2014, p. A16.

en.wikipedia.ord/wiki/2011_Tohoku_earthquake_and_tsunami
.

en.wikipedia.ord/wiki/Fernand_Braudel.

en.wikipedia.ord/Typhoon Haiyan – Wikipedia, the free
encyclopedia.htm.

Personal communication with Tacloban Vice-Mayor Jerry T.
Yaokasin, June 9, 2014.

Thoreau, Henry David. *Walden and Other Writings*. New
York: Barnes & Noble Books,
        1993.

Tolstoy, Leo. *War and Peace* (Oxford World's Classics
paperback). New York: Oxford
        University Press Inc., 1998.

United States Coast and Geodetic Survey. *Map of Leyte, No.
19*. 1899.

www.google.com. Used as search engine for the dates and
other details of disasters that
        struck Visayas and Mindanao in recent years.

www.rappler.com/MAP Strongest earthquakes in the
Philippines.htm.

www.rappler.com/Post-Haiyan-Tacloban-Declaration.htm.

Chapter 6

RICARDO A. ABAN

MY STORY OF SERVICE

My name is Ricardo A. Aban. I am the Stake *(Diocese)* President of The Church of Jesus Christ of Latter-day Saints. I am responsible for thousands of our flocks in the southern region of the Philippines. I am married to Mae Daclan-Aban a self-employed and full-time housewife and mother to five children. Namely Shinehah Mari aged 10, Shemaiah *(deceased)*, Sophia Mia 7, Samantha Faith 5 and Samuel Jacob who was a month old when super typhoon Haiyan *(local name Yolanda)* hit us.

Since our congregation is unpaid clergy, I worked professionally as a full-time Diagnostic Nurse at Eastern Visayas Regional Medical Center (EVRMC) in order to sustain for our daily needs. The EVRMC is a tertiary, training, government hospital that caters to the poorest among the poor in the entire region. And this is my story:

As a nurse by profession, my orientation was providing service to humanity. I was among the few who stayed in the country and deferred any plan for working overseas so I could serve our countrymen. At some point, I decided to leave and look for a greener pasture. But something happened to make me reconsider my decision. The senior brethren from the church came to our place; they interviewed me and told me *"Brother Aban, you have to set aside your personal plans, for the Lord has a plan for you."*

On May 29, 2011, I was called and designated to preside over Tacloban Philippines Stake, a responsibility that I felt I was not qualified. First, I was raising a young family; second, I was in the middle of pursuing promising professional career advancement and third, I felt mediocre since there were others more qualified and experienced to lead our stake, and whose lives were set. However, a passage from the Scripture, *"The Lord uses the simple to bring about His mighty works and purposes,"* gave me the strength and helped me decide to stay and serve the church.

I grew up observing my family's dedication to the church and how they diligently perform the various callings assigned to them. Since we never went to a formal training, we learn about leadership on the job and from frequent leadership trainings. During these trainings, I was taught that as a church leader, most of my efforts are needed to be focused on ministration rather than administration. This meant that I have to delegate some tasks to my subordinates so I could have time for my ministerial responsibilities. I'm glad to have been surrounded by many great men and women who performed to the best of their abilities so they could accomplish our goals and objectives of our organization.

Since I came from the health sector, I encouraged the congregation to help the church and the community by conducting a series of blood donation drives, medical missions, orientation regarding the advantage of getting health insurance, whether personal or government sponsored, and many more.

With the help of wonderful friends, we were also able to invite experts from outside Tacloban City to come train our people on entrepreneurship with the objective of elevating not only their spiritual lives but their temporal lives as well. It became one of the most exciting moment for the church, seeing the awakening of the members' potential and how they would be able to harness several opportunities surrounding them. Many had started to create enterprise and in turn, bless others by creating job opportunities.

While we were engaged in this great cause, a strong earthquake hit central part of the Visayas. Many lives were lost; infrastructure was destroyed; homes were shattered and majority of the people were in dire need of help. One day, I had a meeting with several priesthood leaders from the church and we decided to gather resources so we can bring relief to the destitute. We scheduled to depart for our humanitarian trip on November 29, 2013.

However, few days later, an unusual weather update surfaced, warning us about the super typhoon coming our way. We are a typhoon-prone area and had grown up with the previous typhoon experiences. People thought it would be just another storm and that after it occurs, they would just sweep away the fallen debris and repair the damages it might cause. There was no amount of warning that could scare us even if the local weather bureau would place our area under signal number 4 and the storm as category 5.

I recalled that about 15 years ago as a young missionary in Guam, USA, I witnessed how super typhoon "Paka" tore the entire place apart wiping out the whole island. If not because of their strong houses built to be bomb proof since US military bases are situated in Guam, there would have been many casualties. To my surprise, no one was harmed, except the trees which looked like somebody of great force uprooted them. I told myself that if this will happen in our place, many will perish. Days before the super typhoon hit, I searched super typhoon "Paka" in Google and had learned that the wind gustiness sustained 215 kph only. I was alarmed then because the approaching storm, which was still building up in the Pacific was expected to blow at least 285 kph.

Immediately, we instructed our members to evacuate to our chapels and open its doors to our non-member neighbours. I gave instruction to the bishops to mobilize their quorums and auxiliaries to assess the readiness of our members and to prepare their 72 hours survival kits. Two days prior to the expected date of the typhoon's landfall, many members of the church and their non-member friends started bringing with them their provision. On the evening prior to the storm, my family and I moved to one of our chapels and set up our own command center so I can account and monitor the number of members who I presumed were in the safe haven. Even our leaders in the Area office, who were alarmed too, were giving us the latest development and updates. I sensed how concerned they were of our welfare. I communicated with our local leaders, giving them instructions from time to time.

On the early morning of November 8, 2013, super typhoon Haiyan *(local name Yolanda)* entered the Philippine Area of Responsibility (PAR). The wind was already building up and Haiyan was expected to make landfall at around 4 am. Just as I was exchanging text messages with our leaders in the area office regarding the latest update, the power went out and communications were down, leaving us isolated from the outside world. At the height of its beating, we heard the deafening and eerie whistling sound of the wind. People started to feel a great deal of anxiety. I asked them all to gather and kneel so we could pray to ask comfort from on High and His divine intervention. We let the women, elderly and the children stay in the strongest part of the building while I and the rest of those able men and women kept our post to protect our children and families from the storm. Because the building we were in was sturdy, we were less traumatized even though the roof and ceiling from both 1st and 2nd floors were badly damaged. Rain water dissipated inside the building and window glasses were shattered but then again, flood waters were unable to get inside the building and structurally the building held its ground. It was a great miracle indeed.

Moments after the typhoon, our feelings were ambivalent; we rejoiced with thankful hearts that we endured the strongest typhoon in the history of the planet that made landfall. But we also felt deep sadness because many people had died. The entire city sustained severe damaged, people were in the state of shock. In many places in Tacloban City, there were mountain-like piles of rubble, unclaimed bodies lying everywhere, homes swept out, buildings and infrastructures crumbled people were helpless. The place was in terrible mess. I even wonder how we could be able to bounce back.

Wide scale looting occurred in various commercial establishments and warehouses, even the department stores and malls, were not spared. The need to survive has overpowered morals and values among city residents. I witnessed both men and women, young and old, rich and poor were all equal in the situation. The prices of basic commodities skyrocketed and supply was very scarce.

My first step was to account our members. I learned that we had few casualties from our ranks. They were those who had chosen to stay in their homes. All that evacuated in the chapels were safe and accounted for. However, we needed more supply to sustain our needs since the provision we have prepared for Haiyan was not much.

My next priority was ensuring that our food supply would sustain our needs in the long term since these are scarce and could not be replenished immediately. I instructed everyone to gather our provision and be frugal and wise in dispensing them. It was a good thing we had previous preparation for our departure to Bohol that definitely was canceled because a great calamity came to us. It struck me that we might have been inspired to prepare for the worst to our greater advantage. Since we were unable to communicate outside Tacloban City, we were left to fend for ourselves. This situation encouraged as to be united. Never have I seen a group of people so harmonious in all the things that we do.

Finally, the third day I was able to made contact to our families and friends outside Tacloban and communicated with the church office in Manila. Everybody was anxious of our condition since what happened headlines the everyday news both local and international. Most were dependent on satellite images only and were horrified of the widespread devastation in the area. Many leaped for joy when they learned of our safety; it was a moment where I reflected how special we were as a people.

During this time I came to know that the most important things in life were not the earthly possession you accumulated but the gift of life, your loved ones dear to you like family, relatives and friends, and your relationship to that Divine up there that knows what is best for you.

I'm glad to have a very patient, understanding, loving, and supportive family. My wife who had just delivered our only boy just a month before the typhoon struck never complained. She did not seek special attention and time as she understood the great responsibility I was tasked to administer. She even encouraged me to be resilient and look after the welfare of the majority. My children were equally supportive to their mother.

They found grace in witnessing how their father is in the service of many, setting aside the comfort they might enjoy if we abandon the place and turn our backs from the call I was asked to comply. I am confident that they never thought of leaving the city because we had exposed them to providing service to their fellowmen at an early age. Often times, in the past, I asked them to participate in my relief projects so that they can feel the joy of sharing and eventually become selfless.

In exchange, an outpouring support came to us; only that we had to pick them up at the closest open ports. With the help coming from friends and families, our provision was sustained and I was able to gather enough resources for our people. They also came to check on us and looked after our needs. I gathered resources, driving practically with companions almost 12 hours every day going back and forth in the entire region, leaving very early morning and risking our safety as we travel back to base even late at night. I never felt tired of going about these errands I felt magnified and strengthened. I, too, admire the diligence of our Bishops and several priesthood brethren and many sisters who worked hand in hand, shoulder to shoulder together with us. I was tasked with gathering supplies while the rest distributed these, making sure that no one went hungry.

The church had been very mindful and generous to us. The church made sure that our needs and even wants were attended to. I was certain that our members' needs were met but my prayers included others even to our non-member brothers and sisters. I said to myself that I am not only a Stake President of our church but to all the people that covers the Stake where I was called to preside, and this includes our non-member brothers and sisters. But how could I do it? The limited resources we had were just enough for church members and there was too little to spare. Still, my duty and obligation didn't stop there. I am still responsible to all especially those who needed help.

One day, I received a phone call from a stranger. I wondered how he was able to know me and acquire my contact information. His name was Michael Andrew Schifler, a disaster expert from Hawaii. Michael Andrew was a returned missionary who had served in Moscow, Russia. He was present in such calamities as the strong hurricane Katrina and Sandy, Tsunami in Japan, huge earthquake in Haiti and many more. He invited also Taylor Stockwell, a former missionary here in Tacloban some 20 years ago, to accompany him. Later on, Taylor became my personal assistant and secretary. Schifler came to offer his self, his service, and his resources. I was uncomfortable at first because I cannot guarantee his safety but he was persistent.

I was surprised to learn on the day he arrived that Schifler had wide network. We went to meet a group of people and they were foreigners. When they asked me to lead the relief operation and sought my assistance to facilitate hosting several big names in the disaster expert rooster, it blew my mind. I was also in charge of huge bulk of relief goods to be given to everyone. With the help of generous donors and the collaboration of the kind hearted Salvation Army, they came as an answer to my prayers.

At the course of our relief operation I found favour in these guys. We were able to generate tight friendships and great bond for a very short period of time. On top of distributing resources, I, together with Taylor, attended several cluster meetings with several local and international relief aid agencies. During the cluster meetings, we exchanged ideas with these intelligent men and women and experts in their field. Just few days short of four weeks, we were able to distribute 1.8 million meals with the help of Michael and the amazing Salvation Army.

On the other hand, Taylor initiated micro financing where people with great business potential avail loans so that they could become self-reliant. He had also laid down a great framework of shelter program and system of food distribution. What a great accomplishment indeed. I came to understand that if we trust God and submit to His will, then the very righteous desire of our hearts will be granted to us. He will always make a way for us to accomplish these.

A newly organized department of the church came to make Tacloban a nucleus of their future proponents. Composed of mentors, experienced business people and corporate individuals, they were very concerned of the self-reliance condition of the survivors. They came to determine what assistance they could offer. Tony San Gabriel, a renowned figure in corporate and business development, headed the department. They have yet to launch the Self-Reliance Department of the church with the objective of increasing the economic condition of the members were Tacloban will become a model. During our first meeting I raised this sentiment; *"How could I be comfortable as a provider and head of the family while working outside trying to look for our means, I left behind my family that needed a safe, secured and dignified home?"* I noted that many people were still living in makeshift tents and salvaged materials surrounded with rumours of security threats.

As they shift gears and with diligent collaboration, the idea of the shelter project emerged. A prominent church figure, Bishop Gary Stevenson from the church general headquarters, revolutionized the direction of the welfare system and the church program of self-reliance into one single direction instead of going to opposite sides in the previous practice. His visit became instrumental in the funding of the construction of more than 3,100 transition homes. Under the program, beneficiaries attended a basic carpentry training course on site. After completing the building of five homes, including their own, they were paid for their work.

As time went on, many more responded to help. Several generous individual donors sent their help. Boxes of goods arrived to us that I equally distributed to members. Even monetary gifts were used to fund Christmas parties and other activities as I don't want to rob our children their most anticipated day of the year. We wanted them to move on and by having fun activities they can in turn forget momentarily the horror they experienced during the super typhoon.

However, we are mindful of others too. With the help of the Mormon Helping Hands Volunteers, we were able to distribute thousands of hygiene kits and bags of clothing to several individuals and families living in tent cities, relocations sites and many barangays.

We even hiked up the mountains just to reach the middle of the valley were the Manobo tribe resides. I often saw them being neglected and denied of the relief goods that were due to them. We carried heavy load of relief goods as we climbed a steep mountain but it was worth it as we saw the smiles and expression of gratitude coming from this minority.

Aside from the distribution of clothing and hygiene kits, I am busy in the construction of communal comfort rooms, a project funded from generous donors. More than a dozen of these facilities will be built around the typhoon area. The communal comfort rooms will compose of six cubicles with tiled floor and wall and well painted. There will also be two separate rooms for male and female with two toilets and 1 shower room. During one of the turn-over ceremony that we had in Tacloban, City Councilor Niel Glova who was present during the event said; *"This is by far the first Communal CR project built in Tacloban City even before Yolanda, I'm glad I was able to witness this event."* The Communal CR Project was an answer to the donor's vision of restoring the dignity of the typhoon victims by helping them meet their needs. We not only constructed Communal CR in the barangays but we have built a few in public elementary schools.

Several months have passed since super typhoon Haiyan (Yolanda), the strongest typhoon recorded in our history, occurred but the opportunity to help others never ceased. The stories of how we (Taclobanons) as a people survived the calamity and of our resilience as a people, have inspired others. I continue to abide the admonition of King Benjamin when he said; *"When ye are in the service of your fellow beings ye are only in the service of your God."* With a strong determination I know we can overcome whatever challenges may come upon us. Thus I boldly say *"MAKAKATINDOG KITA TACLOBAN" (We can rebuild Tacloban).*

Chapter 7
RONALD O. REYES

"I WRITE SO THE WORLD WILL NOT FORGET"

By Ronald O. Reyes, Journalist and Yolanda/Haiyan survivor

Ronald, 38, is a freelance journalist based in Tacloban City, Philippines. He writes mainly for the country's daily broadsheet Manila Standard Today; correspondent at UCA News, a Catholic news source based in Bangkok, Thailand; reporter/columnist at Leyte Samar Daily Express, and staff writer of 8 Magazine all based in Tacloban City. He is married to Eden, a radio broadcaster now a city government worker in Tacloban. They have one daughter, Cherub. Ronald also teaches at a local school in the nearby town of Palo, Leyte. About four days after super typhoon Haiyan hit Tacloban on November 8, 2013, Ronald was forced to move his family to Cebu, which was also hit by an earthquake. He and his family arrived in Manila on board the military cargo plane C-130 and there he continued filing reports about his beloved city until his entire family finally returned to Tacloban on January 13, 2014 to rebuild their lives and for Ronald to document about what happened during those difficult days.)

Apocalypse arrived and the great escape

On early Thursday afternoon (November 7), I was at our Leyte Samar Daily Express publication office in Zamora Street, downtown Tacloban, filing my reports (which of course didn't see print the following day).

Thursday evening, our family (I, my wife, and my 8-year old daughter Cherub) decided to evacuate from our house in Caibaan, a village about 2 kilometers away from the city, to Padre Burgos street downtown where my sister-in-law's family lives.

We packed some clothes and food and stayed there because we believed that it was best for us to be intact in one place when typhoon arrived. Just like my family, my sister-in-law's family has only three members (comprising her partner, a young Filipino-Chinese businessman Hector Hui; my sister-in law Delmarie; and their first son Henry, who is of the same age as my daughter). They have one house helper, a cousin named Rose.

They live at a rented two-storey house with the ground floor used as internet computer shop and the second floor as their residence.

We said our family prayer, had an early dinner, and listened to the typhoon updates for the rest of the night while the children went to bed, hugging tight their stuff toys.

While keeping myself abreast of the typhoon on cable TV, my wife, Eden, 34, also did some live phone-reporting to the two local radio stations 531 DyDW-Radyo Diwa (her former employer for seven years) and DyBR, updating the people with the reports coming from city disaster officials.

On ABS-CBN evening TV news edition, we saw Ted Failon, former broadcaster from the city and now working in a giant TV network in Manila, already positioning himself and his crew at the Leyte provincial capitol grounds interviewing Leyte governor Dominic Petilla on the updates and preparations of the province regarding the typhoon.

I have also heard that several national and global news agencies and some internationally-known storm chasers were already checking in at some hotels nearby our place that day.

"Everyone's here. This is for real!" I told myself.

Somewhat foolishly contemplating on it, I posted on my Facebook account: Waiting for Godot, *er,* Yolanda. Then Yolanda or Haiyan came with a mighty wrath.

My wife continued doing radio reports from time to time until about 5:30 a.m. on November 8 when the wind started to blow hard around the city and finally knocking off the electricity and telecommunications facilities, signaling also that every household is on their own now.

Inside, we started to group ourselves, trying to calm each other particularly the children. Remembering one Internet article I read about coping children's fear, I grabbed some stuff toys for my little girl Cherub and for her cousin Henry to at least comfort them while the wind and the rain were pounding hard outside.

As being cheerful is innate to children, the two tried to outdo each other in singing cartoon songs they've learned on TV and doing other tricks, totally unmindful of death stalking outside. Indeed, seeing the two of them seemingly having the "usual good time" brought a sense of relief to us.

About 6 a.m., we decided to move downstairs because we thought the wind could blow off the roof of the building anytime soon.

Downstairs, we started to notice the water making its way into every crevice of the door and windows, then eventually gushing and rushing inside the house. The waters also started rising. Upon seeing the inflow of the water, the women panicked. Hector and I first tried to slow down the entry of the water by placing two large bed foams at the front door. In the end, the effort was of no use as the water now mixed with debris, hammered on the door, forcing it to open.

Floodwaters quickly went up, giving us no time to save the computers and appliances at the ground floor. The water— murky, greasy and putrid-smelling —already flooded the entire ground floor, reaching about 8 feet high.

We went upstairs and all stayed in one room for a couple of minutes until another strong wind blew of the roof. That was the time we realized we were already trapped. With rising flood water downstairs and strong wind blowing above our heads, the situation demanded one's survival instinct to spring into action.

Wasting no time, I then grabbed a mallet (Thank you God, for having that mallet just within my sight and my reach that exact moment) and smashed the back window, so we could escape.

The tall structures surrounding the back of the two-storey house must have prevented the wind from directly slamming us as we made our escape by twos, hand in hand towards a nearby four-storey building.

We made our escape atop galvanized iron sheets roofing of our neighbors' houses amid the wind whirling on us and the rain soaking us.

Upon reaching the four-storey building, I began hammering the thick glass window panel on the second floor so we can get inside. When the owner of the building saw me hammering the thick glass panel, he opened it for us and bid us to enter. We thanked the couple Ramon and Rose Lledo for allowing us to evacuate at their building. There also, Cherub and Henry continued their singing, as if nothing had happened earlier.

At about 11:15 a.m., the wind started to slow down and the water in streets subsided, returning back to sea.

With my mobile phone and video camera in my hand, I went outside the building where we evacuated and started documenting the aftermath of the typhoon downtown. Then I saw other people doing the same, overwhelmed by the Nature's brutal display of fury for just few hours. While filming, I then realized the enormity of the destruction--terrible and apocalyptic.

Seeing the devastation around me, I then started to fear that the same could have happened in Southern Leyte, where my mother and brother lived. I also thought of my students, friends, relatives, neighbors and colleagues living in other areas.

For the next couple of hours, I walked past mountains of debris as I headed back to our own place in Caibaan, some distance from the city's downtown area.

Along the way I bumped into familiar faces, some limping and bleeding, others just transfixed by the images of devastation around, while others were pulling something from the pile of dirt and debris.

By and by, some city workers, volunteers, and a group of soldiers appeared on the streets to give help.

I saw people shaking hands, thankful that they survived Haiyan's onslaught. Some gave a hug to others who were crying, while others tried to stop those who appeared to be going nowhere to ask them if they were okay.

Words spoken were few and far in between among survivors. Everyone was still in a stage of shock...then anguish.

Clearing of roads and pulling of dead bodies from the ruins became the order of the day.

Upon reaching our house, I saw that its roof was blown away and everything inside was rain-soaked and muddy. After cleaning the house and keeping some of the important belongings inside, I then padlocked the door and walked back towards the city.

As darkness started to blanket the city, I saw many people rushing to the streets, literally filing up its every direction. Fear was visible in their eyes, particularly the mothers who were carrying children. "Hurry" was the word mostly repeated by them. Feeling curious, I decided to ask one and I got a terrifying answer: a tsunami is coming!

Common sense told me that I should run towards the mountain along Apitong village just like what the other people were doing, yet I could not just leave my family in the downtown area.

I have to know if they had also heard about an incoming tsunami. I have to know if they were also running towards the mountain. These thoughts were burning on my head that very moment as I could not call my wife over the phone because the telecommunication signal was down. The only thing I could do was to quicken my step towards the city.

That Friday night of November 8, 2013 was one of those nights when God appeared to blink. It was as if there was someone somewhere with a malevolent plan who was silently pleased to see how men, women and children went frantic, miserable, and helpless on earth for a moment.

Upon reaching the building where we evacuated, I thanked God for seeing again my family intact while they huddled around the bright light emanating from my laptop screen.

Outside, one could hear noises of people hammering some doors or buildings, perhaps with the intention of looting some abandoned properties.

It was this time that I wished that I have a gun to protect my family from any stranger who would barge into the door of the building.

That Friday evening after the storm was one of those evenings when one would wish he was away from Tacloban. The air was eerie, with death, destruction and debris on the background. It was akin to post-World War II Hollywood movies. Tacloban became a wasteland, with the widespread destruction.

As no clear help arrived during the entire evening and the following day, fear, hunger and other forms of lawlessness became widespread.

The following day, Saturday (November 9), I went out again to the streets to gather news materials and interview survivors for my first post-Haiyan story.

"It happened so fast, the water level rose quickly," one survivor said.

Around the city, Tacloban mayor Alfred Romualdez, together with other city workers and the Philippine Army continued search and rescue efforts particularly in coastal areas of San Jose and Anibong districts where many were feared dead.

The city also focused on clearing the DZR Tacloban airport runway, so it would be ready for the arrival of any relief assistance from various humanitarian agencies.

"Almost everyone is on foot. No source of gasoline since all of the gasoline stations are destroyed in the city, thus we need pump to get the gasoline. And we need that help immediately," said city administrator Tecson John Lim during my first interview with him after the typhoon.

Lim added that as of their initial body count on Saturday, casualty had reached about 300; but he expressed fear that death toll would reach higher as more people remained missing since Friday.

"Estimated population in the city when the typhoon occurred is 500,000, with all the hotels fully-occupied," Lim added.

As coordinated relief activities were still unseen on

Saturday, more and more people trooped to the grocery and department stores, begging for entrance to get anything from food, clothing, water and other goods. Out of the goodness of their hearts, some store owners voluntarily opened their stores so people could get supplies to sustain them for a day or two.

Other stores however fell into looters' hands.

As of Saturday afternoon, the city continued deploying their emergency rescue teams, while health workers gave anti-tetanus shots for those who were wounded.

I remember, how, at 6:29 p.m. of Saturday, I filed my first report courtesy of the Department of Social Welfare and Development Office who set up free use of internet and mobile phones powered by generators so survivors can contact their loved ones outside the city.

Post-Haiyan writings

My first post-Haiyan stories came on November 10, 2013, when my editors at Manila Standard Today ran a banner story with my article and additional reports from my colleague Maricel Cruz reporting from Manila and from the wires.

As days went by in Tacloban, I and my wife started discussing about leaving the city for a while. Yet along our talks, we also found ourselves both hesitant on the idea of leaving our house and other belongings there. Personally, I also felt that I have to stay behind as there were many stories needed to be told from the ground zero.

On Monday (November 11), about 11 p.m., Hector sent us a driver to fetch us for DZR airport, about 7 km away from where we evacuated down town.

It was a moonless night and the air was filled with putrid smell of dead bodies trying to force its way to our nostrils, causing me to throw up.

We finally decided to leave Tacloban for the health and safety of our little girl.

The trip aboard an improvised motorcycle from downtown area to the airport in San Jose district was so heart-wrenching.

We drove past dead bodies mostly of mothers and children embracing each other, which we saw from with the beam from the motorcycle's headlight.

I did not want my daughter to have memories of this grisly sight so I covered her eyes and told her to go to sleep. A group of soldiers were also seen holding check points from every corner lighted by burning car tires on the streets.

It was a long trip going to the airport. When we reached the airport terminal, we were filled with gladness when we saw the relatives of my wife Jun and Bebe Panis and their children who were also planning to escape the city on board military cargo planes C-130s.

The terminal was a scene of destruction. Except for the air control tower, the rest of the area was in rubble. We were not able to sleep as the floor was flooded with rain water. We barely have a sheet of roof to cover our heads from the rain.

At midnight, electric generators were switched off to save some gasoline.

Early morning of November 12, we rushed to the tarmac along with thousands of other survivors who want to leave the city. The soldiers and international humanitarian agencies were seen everywhere at the airport. The arrival and departure of planes and choppers, big and small, were non- stop.

We lined up and waited until 2 p.m. before we managed to board a C-130 plane. As our plane took off, I felt guilty that we had finally escaped Tacloban while many were still left, desperate at the tarmac. For the first time, I failed one big promise to my little girl: that her first plane ride would be good. Along the way, I guessed she was enjoying the trip also as there were other children on board.

I thanked God we landed safely in Cebu, amid the news of earthquake in the city. We were greeted with relief workers at Mactan Air base. They brought us food, water, medicine, clothing and some toys for the kids. We then waited for another C-130 flight for Manila.

There I managed to type a few sentences on my laptop and sent follow up stories through my mobile phone for my next story regarding our plight.

Joyce Panares, my senior colleague at Manila Standard Today aptly captured our tragic situation when she wrote on November 13, 2013 an article "Mass escape from 'hell'".

After arriving in Manila, I immediately contacted my mother and relatives to assure them that we are all fine. I was happy to know that they have already learned of my safety beforehand as they had been monitoring my news stories since November 8 through the online edition of our newspaper.

I was also glad upon learning that my mother Aurora and brother Arneil in Southern Leyte were spared from the storm.

Help immediately poured in from various individuals and groups to our family. I was also happy that all of my co-workers at school were safe. I however lost two students in one of my subjects.

I tried to settle down and normalize everything for my family in Manila (which includes finding a temporary work for my wife at a call center agency and a school for my little girl).

But I also felt the desire to go back to Tacloban to write more stories of my home city so the world will know and understand our sad plight.

My prayer was immediately answered when my editor Joe Torres of Union of Catholic Asian News (Ucanews.com) in Manila called me on the phone and asked me to be ready to fly back to Tacloban along with two foreign TV journalists from Swedish national television SVT.

From November 18 to November 22, I was fortunate to work with SVT reporter JB Claes Löfgren and his cameraman/photographer Emil Larsson as "facilitator" for their media coverage in Tacloban.

I acted as their planner, interpreter and guide. It was my first time to be a facilitator, and I was glad to know that most of my media colleagues in Tacloban were hired as well by different international news agencies as they scoured for more stories in our city.

To most of my colleagues, they have had found a job again after their respective news outlets were destroyed and rendered unoperational for the time being. It was also sad to know that at least four of our local media colleagues died while on their duty when the storm surge hit their radio stations in Tacloban.

I am thankful to Löfgren and Larsson for they were satisfied with my service. My work with them also helped me regain my financial footing after the storm. I was able to save some money to rebuild our house.

Also by **Cynthia Borgueta-Pease**

The Songs
of the
Unsung Heroes

Also available on
Amazon in
Paperback and
Kindle Edition